SUNDAY AFTERNOONS
WITH TOLSTOY

SUNDAY AFTERNOONS
WITH TOLSTOY

Poems

by

Lynne Burris Butler

Lynx House Press
Spokane, Washington/Portland, Oregon

ACKNOWLEDGEMENTS

The following poems have been previously published: *Prairie Schooner:* "Playing Dead," *Slant:* "Bad Words," *Cimarron Review:* "Reading the Poem," *Half Tones to Jubilee:* "1918," "For My Sister on Vacation from the Oncology Center," "Nothing More to Say," "List of Recurring Dreams," "Lifeguard," "Starting Over," *Prose Poem International:* "Lucy Z," *South Coast Poetry Journal:* "Instructions to the Departing Husband," *Cape Rock:* "The Worst Thing," and *Nightsun:* "Wrestling the Bear"

Library of Congress Cataloging in Publication Data

Butler, Lynne Burris, 1943-
    Sunday Afternoons with Tolstoy : poems /
Lynne Burris Butler.
    p. cm.

PS3552.U82633S86   1999   811/.54 21

ISBN   0-89924-102-6 paper
            0-89924-103-4 cloth

Lynx House Press books are distributed by Small Press Distribution, 1341 Seventh St. Berkeley, CA   94710.

Lynx House Press, c/o 420 W. 24th, Spokane, WA 99203 or 9305 SE Salmon Ct., Portland, OR 97216

for Carol Wolfe Konek
and in memory of Marthann Burris Wright, sisters both

CONTENTS

"Everything I've learned so far
has been wrong."
       —Rick Bass, *Winter*

SUNDAY AFTERNOONS WITH TOLSTOY ——————

for S.

Nothing much happens here
on Sunday.   No mail, no visitors
arrive from the capital.

There are closets that could be cleaned,
shoes and boots grim as a coal scuttle
to be polished, a history

of skirts and blouses to unravel.
There are windows that could be washed,
surfaces where your mother's face

is as persistent as the robin
that flies and flies
into the glass of the storm door.

But perhaps there will be a distraction,
a sudden squall, a branch crashing
onto the porch.   Or maybe

a phone call from my house
to yours to interrupt the afternoon,
the kind of afternoon

when Anna makes perfect sense,
when page after page, the story
doesn't get better, just longer.

"Behold, happy is the man whom God correcteth."
—*Job* 5:17

My students believe the Bible
was written by Moses and David
certainly God himself and most likely
in English one day a long time ago
right after Eve got what was coming
to her. Appalled

              by the cool eye
of scholarship they grip their books
furiously, pencil fences of crosses
in the margins of their papers—
they have made a hedge on every side.
One more word, their eyes warn me,
one more word....

              They step around me,
a stone on the narrow path. They know
what is deserved—for trouble comes not
from the dust. They have their reasons
the smudge pot burns, the vagrant lies,
the sparrow falls from the bough.

In their world there's even a reason
for the shattered living room window
I discovered this morning, a reason
someone stood with a pistol
in the darkened woods beyond my house,
positioning himself just right.

PLAYING DEAD ─────────────

He scared me, or maybe it was a she
possum, dead in my garbage can
a lump of grey fur and the unmistakable

rat tail curled where I expected
to see lettuce or newspapers.
And it wasn't small, that body

to be disposed of on a Monday morning
me in a suit and high heels
annoyed, in a hurry, thinking about

how something succulent,
a chicken bone or heart of palm
left over from an almost successful

dinner party, and the night, probably
one when the dogs put away
their teeth, and the car lights

wore hoods and the drunken kid
in his black Trans AM, the one
who'd never swerve, stayed

on a distant street, how they led to this
climb up the woodpile between the garbage
and the Paul Scarlets, their perfume

and petals no match for the seduction
of the inescapable. Oh, I was worked up
when the eye opened and that faker

death said one more chance, a rescue,
a reprieve, as though it were so simple
to eat our fill, to play dead, to waddle away.

FOR MY SISTER ON VACATION FROM THE ONCOLOGY CENTER ——————————

I don't want to dramatize,
but when you walk into the hotel
Auschwitz comes to mind.
In the midst
of resort technicolor,
you are a still frame
in grey. People stare.
Perhaps, from our whim
of identical tee shirts,
they imagine you are
my aged lover.
You make jokes
about your crew cut hair,
retribution
for years of complaining
about natural curls.
We defy the odds
and doctors' orders
as we drink a glass of wine
knowing tomorrow you must return
to drink the healing hemlock
they prescribe and to sail out
beyond my prompting, alone,
center stage, diva, star,
sister, who leads the way.

That summer when we were briefly
the same size, we traded clothes
the way girls might—my red silk

for your black gauze—our dance cards
filled, my feet following
the steps you taught me.

That last summer while I fussed
over mother-of-the-groom gowns
you kept me going, said one more

dress can't hurt, said it's good
to have a spare, kept saying
doctors don't know everything

until the pain that had been
your secret demanding lover
moved in, set up housekeeping,

seated himself at the head of the table
and without even ringing a little crystal
bell, said "I'm hungry. Let's eat."

Medical
History

She is bald as a turnip and for the first time
in her life has cheekbones arrived
special delivery from breast cancer via
the genetic pool mother to daughter to
sister with a detour to the spine
and brain. She can have morphine
every four hours, Ativan for anxiety
sooner. Decadron for swelling and
Sulfatran twice a day but not
within an hour of milk or
milk products. I watch the clock
as though it might be possible
to catch the wave just right somewhere
between pain and sleep. Sometimes
it is. "I'm forging ahead. Just forging
ahead," she says as though she were
delivering mail to the north pole.

The Wrong
Door

The apartment was on 20th
next to an orchard, a pear orchard.
We could see the tanks in the orchard
learning to maneuver. Sometimes
Mother drove Daddy to the corner
where he caught the bus to the base.
We had to go through the red light
district and she'd make me lie down
on the seat and cover up with a blanket.
Sometimes he caught a different bus
home and I could ride my tricycle
to meet him.

A little girl got lost from the school.
She went out the wrong door
and walked the wrong direction.
They looked for her a long time.

The apartment on 20th was next
to a pear orchard. That wasn't where
I bent over and burned my bottom
on the gas heater. The squares were big,
like chicken wire, no, hog wire, I mean.
I didn't cry because I was afraid
of being spanked. It was the one
near the orchard where we could hear
the tanks at night. I slept on a little
bed in the hall and I could hear the tanks.

Spider

It is a season of phone calls late
night and early morning strands
across the silence we know is coming.
Again last night a garden spider has been
busy. Skeins cross between the dogwood
and azaleas. A hummingbird
intent on migration, the sun whispering
through it's skull, could be caught there,
beached midair, a small flaming sword.

She is weightless these days
as a hummingbird. Her conductor's
hands hover near her mouth
coaxing out words. See. See.
Or perhaps it is C, the note,
middle C somehow grounding her
mid-scale, whatever she holds to.
Her words come to me. *I won't die
just as a convenience.*

Loaded

Meanwhile I tell everyone
off—the old lover, the one
who considered love an abstraction
who offers in the abstract to do anything,
anything at all, should in my opinion,
get a life as his has absolutely

concretely nothing
to do with mine. The student
who wants to leave my class
fifteen minutes early every day
to do something really important
might take a serious look at trade school
because as a scholar and human
being she'd make an excellent
blank wall across from a transients'
hotel. And the nazi next door
who swears he'll shoot my dogs can,
as far as I'm concerned,
go fuck himself or if he prefers
I'll personally drive his dick
into the dirt and p.s. I have friends
with guns. I load my gun
with everything that needs to be said
quick before they're out of range.

The Hospice	*Refusal to eat.*
Nurse Tells Us	At this advanced stage of emaciation
There Are Signs	her hands and face suggest the surface

Refusal to eat.

At this advanced stage of emaciation
her hands and face suggest the surface
of the smoothest lake, her skin
so thin it reveals the smallest minnow.
Where bones bear weight, the skin
splits in new places every day.

The extremities swell.

Her feet are cold. I rub them
remembering my child who
would squirm and giggle
demanding a game of sniffing
his sweet moist toes exclaiming,
"Phew! Stinky!" These little sausage
toes no amount of massage can warm.
On one heel, a discoloration. Something
like the color of a dried rose.

The eyes dry out.
                She is looking at space, air,
                something else.

Tone Deaf   A man tells a story. How his tone deaf
                 wife played the flute, tuned up with the rest
                 of the band by measuring the gap
                 in her instrument against the space
                 the conductor held out to her between
                 his fingers. I am wondering if it worked.
                 I'm wondering if it is a skill that can be learned.

God's   "I ask God to please help me see what I'm
Classroom   supposed to learn from this."
                                        —her husband

                 You know I don't buy what
                 they say. So let's skip the incense
                 and bloody knees. Try to think
                 of me as that student who sits
                 in the back and looks like he should be
                 selling used batteries at a flea market
                 but still manages somehow to pass
                 the test. Or maybe as the one who
                 offers up like a prayer the excuse
                 "I did the best I could."

                 Your aide-de-camp says he believes
                 in the communion of saints, in this case,
                 a chipping sparrow who hinted reassurance to him
                 in his father's voice. An idea with some
                 appeal except for certain textual
                 difficulties. Don't forget end of semester
                 evaluations are coming. You're getting a bad score
                 from me on number and difficulty of assignments.

Stories   *My brilliant wondrous*
                 sister. Brilliant stories
                 She can tell brilliant stories.

We are anecdotal, this family.
What story does she want? The cocker
spaniel who buried toast in the privet hedge?

The father who nailed our Christmas trees
to the wall? Why not how I rescued my
dog who thought he could swim to Cuba.

He had gone a good way before I knew
I'd have to swim for it, I, modestly,
in a public place not wanting to strip out
of my clothes and he acting like a wind up
duck about to disappear over the horizon.

This is a funny story, hilarious, really,
until you get to the part where I realize
I can't lift my arms out of the water
and that I can't kick out of my jeans, that the dog
may bite me even if I can get to him, that I
could sink into this brown water and not even the dog
would know that I had gone through the wrong door.

But in this version I'll be a graduate Red Cross junior
lifesaver, or maybe Esther Williams trailing seaweed.
This time the dog obeys; Fernando Lamas wraps
us both in a blanket. In this version, a trip to Cuba
seems like a good idea. Be more careful. You must
be more careful. Her voice sinks. She is bone
weary. As weary as someone who has swum
across a lake in stone shoes.

Whisper

Whisper on me.
Whisper on me.
I need kisses.
I drove and drove.
I need kisses.

Fog wraps the house.
Even her velvet cat
who stares through the glass
doors for hours gives up
stalks to another room.
At this hour only the call
of a barred owl confirms
that anything moves.

Help me. Help me.
I want to go home.

It's too soon for morphine
do not tell this to a poet
but who will know.
Swallow. Swallow this.
Let my hands be easy
as fog on her face. Let
my words be soft
as the wings of owls.

Whisper on me.

Her hands flutter at her throat
small birds against a glass.

It's okay. Just float toward home.

But vital signs. I have no vital signs.

Let my lips do what is right.
Let me whisper what is needed.
You have driven far.

REMEMBERING YOU IN THE CITY OF THE HONORED DEAD ———————————

Your absence has become
a daily commute, growing
longer but a little automatic
knowing when to shift lanes
or what hours to avoid. Grief
picks its times. It is
cummulative. An old city,
it builds outward, the suburbs
nudging each other into the innocent fields.
It sprawls and grows comfortable
until we scarcely notice
the new by-pass we had to build
just to make our way home.

At its heart are the tight seeds
of the thousands of dead,
each name a box,
each marking the enormity
of what we know too late.
In the city of grief,
the homeless woman
in the doorway protesting
the indecency of automobiles
must surely pass through the streets
slowly, perhaps so slowly
she sees only the discarded shoe,
the flattened bottle cap.

She has learned to see things
separately. She has learned to avoid
her reflection in the windshields.

CHORUS LINE ──────────────────

> "If only we could climb into a photograph..."
>
> *—Anne Tyler*

What would I tell them,
my glamorous sister, a buxom
teenager in a strapless top

posed with one shapely leg
pointed, worrying,
as she always did

that she looks fat, but
who is lucious, really,
as a starlet

if we overlook the muddy loafers
she is inexplicably wearing
this August afternoon.

Or what might I say to my plump
and freckled mother whose peasant
blouse and crumpled slacks

suggest off-hand happiness,
her smile oblivious to the trouble
that leans against her like bookends,

these daughters she links
arms with in someone's idea
of a chorus line.

Mostly, I wonder what I'd tell
the ten year old me, body
all twigs and determination

baggy shorts and a blurred shirt,
cheesecake pose and a 300 watt smile
that could audition for the Rockettes.

What a trooper this kid is
in the face of weeds growing
through the sidewalk,

Dutch elm disease,
and a photographer who cuts
her left arm out of the picture.

Maybe I'd tell her to get in the Buick
that seemed always to be planted
in the background and keep on driving

because who'd have the nerve
to tell her nobody can tap dance
forever or even mention the fact

that next week there will be
an unexplained fall, that
they'll cut the blouse from her,

a blouse, I remember now,
that was printed with love letters
and sprinkled with tiny red hearts.

UNDERGROUND ———————————

He says nothing. Absolutely
nothing. He doesn't want to talk
about it. He has nothing to say.

His teeth are bricks in a wall.
Behind it is a yard where words
hang like wash on a line

slowly freezing dry. All
his ideas have gone underground,
are classified, secret.

He doesn't dream, or if he does
they mean nothing. At night
the light stays on in his head,

a lamp at the end of a dead end
street. Nothing passes.
Nothing moves.

She considers the options:
perhaps chisels, a well placed punch
to the solar plexus. Her fingers

probe his throat, find a fragment,
a phrase, pull deftly a rabbit
from a hat, then flowers, scarves, a string

of paper dolls, words cut
from a page, a thread of clues
going hand in hand.

She hangs the dolls between two chairs,
turns on a fan and they dance
cheek to cheek. Palmettos

clatter in the background.
Pink parrots, gulahs are flying now
among the vines that twine

around the words that blossom.
"Hello," they say.
"Hello. Is anybody there?"

BAD WORDS ─────────────────────────

As though Martians had invaded,
Lincoln School glowed ultraviolet
at night and during the day the latest thing,

an air sanitizer, killed our germs
faster than you could say polio
or meningitis, not to mention

colds, pink eye, ring worm,
all the bad things that could happen
if you didn't watch your step, watch out

for trick questions, the misery
of multiplication tables, or the spelling
words hurled like hard packed snowballs.

Stubborn or *dividend*, or even
an easy one like *rabbit* could trip me up,
leave me stunned,

reeling, dumb, and banished
from the blackboard to the empty rows
of desks, the gulag of failure.

No solace for a dunce like this,
not even art class where the teacher patrols
behind us, emphasizing color and composition,

who snatches my fragile sketches
of a house with wisps of smoke
drifting from a chimney, tiny lace curtains

at the orderly windows, a house
wherein a mother makes fudge and sits
at the kitchen table singing out words

turning the whole list into a familiar tune
until the Inspector General breaks down
the door shouting, "You see? No color. Nothing."

Walking home, desperate and suddenly
reckless, I take the dare to walk
through the culvert that runs under Canal Street.

After all, it's safe enough,
no flash floods in sight, and the bayonet
at my back is only the echo

of my own footsteps and the taunts
scaredy cat a scared little rabbit
running straight for the teeth

in a concrete tunnel where somebody
has drawn peculiar pictures and painted
the word pussy and others I don't know

but clearly words so bad,
so unimaginably dangerous,
they could be written only underground.

THE WORST THING

Swapping tales
we tell all, almost.
Such stories
where the worst thing
is that someone finds out
lull like the gin
we swallow them with.
In my turn
I'm cast adrift
into the current of a resort town
with a friend so eager
to melt into the holiday
version of herself
that we're picked up
like pieces of driftwood
by the first boys
we meet on the main drag.
Or she is.
I'm carried along,
flotsam on this adventure
as the car edges through the pines
and we feel our way toward the dare,
the jimmied window
of the house of people
whose name you'd know
where we roved with candles
through rooms of furniture
wrapped in dust sheets
fingering the objects
of a grander life.
I remember
the teapot and cups
she tucked in her purse,
the flicker of light
on bare mattress ticking.
I remember
she begged me not to tell.

The second Thursday
of every month we dressed
in tulle, nylons, garter belts,
fake pearls, maybe gloves,
and went downtown upstairs over
Duckwalls 5 & 10 to the mysteries
of the Masonic Temple, the sacred
East, for rituals mostly involving
square corners and speeches
aimed at turning us
into fine young women.

When I tell you this,
I want you to see how afterwards
we rushed down the wide staircase
to our boyfriends who kept
the motors running. I want
you to hear the net skirts,
a sound like wind ruffling
a wheat field and to feel
how smooth the wide silver
bannister was beneath our hands.

Oh, there were rules:
no blacks, no Catholics, no girls
whose fathers owned liquor stores,
no smoking and come straight
home on school nights,
but as we swept into the night
our words were the sudden
chatter of goldfinches flushed
from a meadow, our laughter
jangled the stars though
in the cars we sat close to the boys
docile as bowls of milk.

And if the dresses were second-hand
or homemade, still
we were elegant, almost
women, armor hard bras
carrying our breasts like bijouterie,
little jewels his fingers
crawled toward until I wanted
to grab his hands and say Here.
Here. But that was not
the way out for a rainbow girl
who had her eye on the east,
maybe Wichita or even Kansas City.

He was nine years old, small
for his age because there was no food,
wearing overalls, no coat, a sweater

when he left half his money,
fifty cents, for his mother
and the baby and hopped a box car.

It is easy
to pity that child
but it doesn't change anything.

If I could love a child
who could do that,
if I could send love back

like a care package blanket
to wrap him before the cold
settled permanently in his bones,

it would not stop
the dark shapes that rose
from the corner, from the rattling

racket that hid everything and ripped
trust and courage out of that boy,
seized him and took him, tossed him out

like an empty sack beside the tracks.
It would not send me a father
who ever picked himself up.

Sister, they called her, until she went to school and Teacher said that wasn't a name, what was her name? And she had none, so she named herself Lucy Z. No daddy either except the one who disappeared and the other Mamaw sent away. But still she had Lloyd and George Ward and Baby Don who all became railroad men, who rode the tracks way out west. So she bought herself a ticket out of that old turtle of a town and went to Memphis, oh southern girl of pecan pies and a good fur wrap, and she studied nursing and got a taste for more, then flew away to California where she met Mary Pickford who gave her a vase of glazed grey porcelain and she had a lover who bought her everything, rings, a belt with silver conches, and begged her to marry him, to move to Nebraska or somewhere like that, but of course she wouldn't which is why she gave me the belt saying, "Oh, it's just something." And she bought Waterford crystal at an antique auction, pieces so fine we'd look for years and never find another and she'd say, "Let's have a toddy for the body," before dinner on her brilliant Chinese plates. "I wouldn't trust a woman whose dishes all match," she taught me. And she loved my husband and adored my son and when they were in the room, I'd disappear one two three into the trick trunk of the unimportant, the insignificant to Lucy Z who had made herself a woman of style.

GOOD WIFE

after Chagall's "Double Portrait With A Glass of Wine"

How wonderful to float on or just
above a good wife's shoulders.

She is substantial, this woman.
Those breasts invite hands and lips

and her feet, slender as willows,
are firm on the grass of the foreground.

And you in a red coat and a green vest
are so happy that your face slips

away from your shoulders as though you
were a little drunk on life or the wine

you salute us with. Even the sun
has gone adrift and meanders off

the left side of the canvas, out of reach
of the baby, a tadpole, a polliwog

who somersaults above it all, who certainly
is destined to be an olympic airborne gymnast,

who will win prizes, flowers, accolades
of the very angels. Oh love! Oh joy!

Before gravity sets in. Before the good wife
reminds you that the consequence of wine

is a headache. Before you deduce that the apple
falls not from the tree for love of the ground.

Before, like the baby, you all learn to say no
in a land where the sun stays firmly in place.

READING THE POEM

is like the day your lover
gets home late and smells
like he's taken up smoking
again and you go on
to the next day and
don't think much about it
but you notice his mouth
when he kisses you
feels like a letter
addressed to occupant
and the days inch by
doing the two step
and you're counting
the times he forgets to call
and remembering how when
he does call the words
hang around your head
like a cloud of gnats
and you start waking up
in a dream where all
the road signs say One
Way or Closed Permanently
Under Water in a landscape
where nothing looks quite familiar
and you refold the map
and see this is where
you were headed
all along.

> "Sometimes the past is lurking around corners,
> and lying in wait for us, like a bridge."
> —*Edward Hirsch*

1.   When you were bad,
oh, very bad, pinching
your sister's arm blue, crying
under the taunts of your older
brother or when the three of you
combined, joined forces
to drive your mother mad,
she'd disappear to the basement.
"I'm leaving you," she'd warn.

           How you all laughed
sitting around holiday tables,
the turkey breast cut bare
to the bone, your mother's face
flushed with protest
each of you struggling
to have the last word.

           You walk out
of our bedroom, a suitcase
in your hand. "I'm leaving"
you say, "before we kill
everything."

2.   The forest
propped up in the vacant lot
could be the steppes of Russia,
our old Chevy station wagon
a sleigh with tarnished bells,
but it's only Wichita
in the sixties at twilight
on a Friday as the air
thickens with snow.

You choose
a Douglas fir, your favorite
and more than we can afford.
A man I imagine I could love
is having his third beer
across town at the Why Not
unaware of how splendid
I look in my Salvation Army
seal skin coat, as you and I
are unaware of something indigenous,
the long muzzle of something
there just beyond the twinkling
lights of Christmas yet to come.

3.   As I remember

it was a cross
between a tree house

and a crow's nest,
the apartment on the second story

of the house that loomed
toward Gilbert street

where the ratty lace curtains
sifted dust and the trees

beyond the windows sifted
leaves and light

in those few minutes
before I left to ride the bus

weeping over old men
in torn sweaters or returned

in the last gritty remnants
of winter afternoons

where you taught me
to shape up to fold not roll

your socks and where
from the rooms below

a strange and onerous smell
rose as though the whole world

had died down there
and I alone knew it.

4.   "And then the windows failed and then
I could not see to see."
—Emily Dickinson

I drifted unaware
of the current's ribbons
the loosening of knots,
of you asleep in a chair
beside my bed. *We're losing her.*
We've lost her pulse.

I took notes somewhere
near the ceiling before I tumbled
through a tunnel of diminishing light
before they beat me back
and I opened my eyes and saw
your face as grey as mine,
your hands holding my purple arm.

We weren't mystics. We didn't
even believe the nurse
who told me I was dead.
We preferred the milder version
of the cardiologist who knows
no one comes back from the other side.

But for twenty years we said
If you hadn't been there....
and the closest of calls became
I owe you my life.

5.   I'm too old
to feel like throwing up
in the produce department
of Food World
where we meet by chance
on Sunday morning.

The crazed heart
runs naked through the aisles
as you weigh two peaches
and note the price
of grapes. Our matching baskets
depart: one pound hamburger,
two peaches, a single
Damson plum.

6.   The bed seems smaller
since you left.
It is a boat
without oars
I ride each night.
Of course
there are snags.
A branch scraping the roof.
The dog stirring
in the basement.
Too much wine.
Not enough air.
Stagnant water.
Everywhere
the darkest night
turns and runs.

7. The version
   she tells
   their son:

   The version
   she tells
   his mother:

   The version
   she tells
   their friends:

   The version
   she tells
   herself:

He wouldn't do this
if he didn't have to.

We are apart
(detached disjoined
disconnected separated
split sundered).

He's trying to discover
why he hates his life
I'm trying to be
a good sport about it.

This is where you're hiding
a snug cave
where you can hold off
the kamikaze
world where you've gone
to lovingly rub
the Luger inside
the mouth of forever,
where you practice
tying knots around the neck
of I love, I need, I want,
a family.

8. In which she
   she explains how
   all right she is

I've met 12 new people
All of their chairs match.
Come for a drink, they say
where I listen to their children
punch bruises on the piano.

9. In which she
   says don't call
   me, I'll...

I can't take another midnight
phone call, those crackling
silences rushing toward me
then whining past,
the receding sound
of all we've given up.

It's time.
You can't keep me
like an extra can of tuna fish
just in case.

10. In which she
changes her
mind

Listen: Last night I drove
all the way to Chicago to see you
through construction, traffic
and a department store window
to end up in a phone booth
with your brother who told me
you'd forgiven me.

Have you? And if so, for what?

INSTRUCTIONS TO THE DEPARTING HUSBAND ——

Take everything you will need
for your new life— the many
silences that hung like suits
in your orderly closet,
the reasons you tended carefully
as a garden. Continue to water
them. They will feed you all winter.
Take the past which is obsolete,
a history written by liars,
a canvas you can paint over.
Abandon the guilt you wore
like shoes that pinched
but were too good to throw out.
Refuse to accept the scraps
of affection that still come
your way like misdirected letters
or unordered goods. Unpack
quickly. If the rooms seem
empty, fill the cabinets
with Swiss chocolate, fine wine,
more money. Bolt your door
against the static from yesterday.
Keep moving. Learn nothing.

NOTHING MORE TO SAY ——————

Today the movers take the last of it—
drill press, planer, lathe, the rows
of crescent wrenches each aligned

in perfect order, four hand saws,
levels, squares, the esoteric chisels
that only the finest craftsman

could ever have used. They load it up,
even the brass screws for the birdhouses
that were never built. The table, solid maple,

that took you three years to build
from wood that held it's own light, the one
we struggled to balance boards for,

the one that seated ten at parties,
is gone to storage. The movers wrestle
cabinets, then a band saw past us

and we stand in an empty basement.
That's it. Nothing more
to say. Wrong, as usual.

There will be more to say
in nightly visits, the hurled
accusations, the blows

that never quite reach you.
There will be careening sailboats
where from the mast I scream,

"Are you asleep down there?"
And there will be a lifetime,
graduations, weddings,

grandchildren I'll love alone.
And what of you, heart like a vice,
was this how you meant it to be?

TRUSTING THE FUTURE ───────────

for Alex and Chris
Rice University, Class of '92

From Le Harve the rattle
of coins in a phone box is a token
reassurance from two explorers

who have the world by the tail,
baguettes and wine
for the ferry, and only a little

sore throat and diarrhea, nothing
to worry about, nothing tomorrow
won't fix.   Yesterday

we sat in a courtyard
beneath banners fanning
the steamy Houston morning

and were promised cooperation,
connection, the dissolution
of walls— the Berlin wall, in fact,

built during the crisis that recalled
your father to active duty
the very day he was to begin college.

It fell, no thanks to him,
and the pieces now enshrined
or sold in shopping malls

take on their own meaning, mean
you travel freely to Bonn
or Berlin, a fact we toast

with long-necks and limes
and buckets of crawfish so hot
our lips burn for hours.

Meanwhile, above the bar
the silent news shows a phalanx
of police advancing on L.A.

and I, mother, worrier, johnny-come-
lately radical, see Kent State,
DaNang, the burned out shell

of Detroit the year you
were just a dream of connection
while the two of you dream

adventure in black and white.
Who could have told the argonauts
that the other side of adventure

is knowing that nothing will ever
be better, or that trouble springs
ever from the dragon's teeth?

I think of Jason, a guy who always
missed the point, who thought
the main chance was down the road,

around the corner. Maybe
in this version he learns to love
the present, lives to a noble old age,

maybe this time somebody
learns the danger of walls
before it's too late. Maybe Medea

thinks better of it,
folds up the napalm of her rage
like a dress she can no longer wear

and sees that the best revenge
is rearing different sons,
ones whose hearts know connections.

It could happen, for even though
the line from LeHarve stutters
over Bon jour, Mama, it holds.

FALSE SPRING ———————————————

Sandwiched between rain
and the approaching cold front,
a day that pulls everyone,

even the worst sluggard
in the neighborhood, out
to mow or plant annuals.

Sun, blessed sun, makes believers
of us though it's too early
by the calendar for such trust.

Three years of neglect

and this yard is a shambles—
the iris want thinning,
the roses are a lost cause.

Pandas or their cousins
the raccoons could be living
in the bamboo thicket.

Only the crab apple tree,
the one that never bloomed,
seems to have it right.

You should see it.

I still get reports,
dispatches from a distant land.
He was dining alone. Why

would anyone drive all that way
to dine alone? I know
the way a character

in *The Dubliners* knows
you hear nothing of me.
But then, why would you?

The news from here is transitory

as the indigo buntings
that paused last week, iridescent flecks
among the rampant weeds.

I glance up. The glint
at the upstairs window, hard as silence,
is nothing, certainly not your wave,

your summons, I'm home. The wind
shifts and the bamboo leaves rustle,
swift as water in the Wei He gorge.

It's cold, time to go in, to put our trowels away.

SUMMER WORK

for Mike

One summer his father got him a job
in the brick factory, a two bit
operation that turned nauseous yellow
clay into the stuff that bungalows,

dreams with bomb shelters, were made of.
A good job, one he was lucky to have,
despite the way the tin roof magnified
the sun, cooking up heat stroke temperatures

in the hopper where he tamped clay
and watched for the inevitable clogs.
Sisyphus could have learned something
seeing how he'd leap into the funnel

to battle the grinder's relentless
maw, a mouth that could take an arm
or leg, or the way he ignored the chance
the clay might shift and pin him there.

It made him thirsty and restless,
something that not even the cool
clink of beer bottles and the pool
tables in the back room of the Blue Moon

could soothe, and at midnight,
he'd hit the road in his souped up car
roaring down gravel roads
alone or more often drag racing,

beating some kid from Great Bend
or beyond. Once he showed me
the hill and straight-away where,
when the moon was bright enough,

they'd race without lights, once
so fast the speedometer slipped
past 120 and stuck, permanently,
or kept on going ever faster,

spinning out in the clear black cosmos,
faster than the speed of light and history
circling back on itself. *It was beautiful*,
he breathed. *Those bald tires would lift*

and we'd fly that whole long summer before
I knew him, before a little sleep, a cup of coffee,
then another day in the brick factory,
another car, another road, another escape.

LIFEGUARD

It was a job made in heaven.
Lifeguard at the country club

pool, a sapphire set at the edge
of the brand new 18th hole,

a real gem of a job with free suntan
and after hours rum and cokes.

Perfect, except for the frogs
that had to be scooped each morning

from the gutters, sullen
little fists that liked to leap

out at me. But really, it was
glamorous, sun streaked hair,

my first two piece swim suit,
a young Esther Williams or maybe

her understudy for an easy part
with one line...Walk! Don't run

and at the end of the day,
exit upstage into the sunset

and drive the dusty three miles
back to town, to your letters

from far off Wyoming, letters
full of grumbling about that summer's

version of war, pointless
marches, endless drill, a lout

of a sergeant. In particular,
I remember your complaints about

grubby hands, food a dog wouldn't eat.
Meanwhile, I counted the days

in my watery world, a naiad,
a teenaged Thetis, lovely

and hopeful before she figures out
what happens next, before

the assistant cook gets drunk and breaks
his neck diving into the wading pool,

before some numbskull goes off
the deep end with the greens tractor

and cracks the concrete shell,
before it all drained away.

CHRISTMAS IN THE BLUE MOON POOL HALL ——

> "Everything I've learned so far has been wrong."
> —Rick Bass, *Winter*

Winter. Christmas Eve, in fact,
the stars, sparks of light struck
against the flint of five below zero.

Behind us, parents who live
in the rubble of dementia—
aluminum pie tins arranged

on every table, a feast of nothing
they can explain, fragments, photos,
odd scraps of fabric my mother

sorts and worries over, saves
from the baby who might tear them.
What ever happened to fudge?

To a tree too big for the tree stand?
To stockings stuffed with surprises
and left us with these lumps of coal,

these words stuck in our throats,
these tumbleweed lives driven
like deer before a blizzard.

Never mind. We know the drill:
Keep sand and a shovel in the trunk.
Never run the motor if stranded.

Be prepared. Stay warm. A blanket
and some hard candy will keep you safe
until help can find you. But no snow

tonight. Just the black dome of sky
and barbed wire fences that sigh
against the miles they must hold back.

Ahead, his parents who live in the static
of recriminations. His father
who cites time and place, transgressions

grown rich as cultured pearls, accusations
his mother fingers, counts, her protests
fluttering against us like trapped pigeons.

No wonder we abandon the baby
and head for the pool hall
where Charlie has festooned

the jack-a-lope with tinsel, where
good cheer flickers like a yule log,
and hope rises green as the neon

behind the bar where a radio searches
for good will toward men, but heralds
down the road, more bad weather.

STARTING OVER ─────────────

It started at night somewhere beyond
Sharon Springs most likely

over the state line in Colorado,
a sour, straightforward wind

that blew steadily for days. "There goes
the wheat crop to Missouri," the men

in the Donut Delight deadpanned, only
it wasn't funny, the way the car lights

became yellow cat eyes in the dim
afternoons and the way grit sifted

through our windows despite wet towels,
masking tape, everything we could think of.

And by night we were beaten, had accepted
the howl beneath the front door

as pioneer women reconciled themselves
to the wolves that prowled their farmyards

sniffing out blood or death, persistent
as this wind that went anywhere it pleased

and left its mark, deposited dust like
a calling card on sheets and chocolate cake,

in our noses and in the slack mouth
of a man asleep in the arms of his wife.

Then it stopped. No reason. No notice.
The muffled tread of tires the next day

could have been the crepe soled shoes of nurses
approaching with news of something too serious

to say aloud, the drifts of dirt
across the backyard smothering

the grass, the town buried alive
until we began to dig out, to re-seed

amid the muttering of vacuum sweepers and
the asthmatic gasp of a tractor trying

to start. Oh, it's just a matter
of starting over, my mother said,

as she watched the tractor scrape away
her garden, the iris and peonies planted

by her mother. Just a matter of cleaning up,
sweeping out, except for something

settled in the grain, something stubborn
and as insoluble as what I later came to know

about starting over when the past has blown
away and you feel scraped bare to the bone.

THE LIST OF RECURRING DREAMS ——————

1. Crossing a bridge covered with water.
2. Attack of insects.
3. Dreams of flying.
4. The examination.
5. Being naked in public.

1.

He offers these casually
but with some amazement
as though they were birds
he had just noticed in his apple tree:
an evening grosbeak,
uncommon in these parts, but still
not unexpected. When he calls from
far upstate he tells the dream
of crossing a bridge covered with water,
water that tumbles treacherously
around his feet but, he reports,
if you look closely you can see clear
to the bottom. I wait for him to see,
but it flits away, elusive,
migratory, determined to fly south.

2.

Something about bees.
Something small and stinging
stubborn and fractious.
Something he forgot
to do whatever he meant
or didn't mean typed out
rapid fire rattling the glass
of every window whispering
insistent in the hive.

3.

Waking in his arms, I dream
his dream. Deer fly across
a field, pirouette recklessly
and disappear. There is a cabin,
the sound of a door slamming
and far away like horns in a muted
symphony, the baying of dogs.

His trophies—antlers, salmon,
mallards—paste themselves
into the pages of my sleep.
Deer camp, a face bloodied
with the mark of a first kill,
his past becomes my future.
He turns away. Silence. Dead
weight hangs between us.

It's heavy work,
this transmigration of souls.

4.

He's missed the test. No—
it's worse than that. He's
missed the course entirely.
He never read the book, doesn't
recognize the formulas, can't
understand a single word
that floats from the professor's
mouth, words that fill the room
like snowflakes, huge, moist
handfuls of snow that settle
on his head and his shoulders,
that pile up around his legs,
deep drifts he struggles through,
his toes and fingers growing numb,
brittle twigs that could snap
in the slightest wind. Where
are his mittens? Is this the way

home? Why are the houses
all dark and the street signs
scribbled in Greek?

5.

Like Adam and Eve caught
knowing too much about the past
we cover the naked truth
as best we can.
"I'm an ordinary man," he says,
wearing the camouflage
of mowed grass and winter greens.
"I'm a good cook," I say,
stitching an apron of flour
and yeast. "I miss you"
we say, a trade for miles
or weeks. We play fair
neither acts the martyr.
Soon disguises not now and love,
this side of the garden,
becomes a matter of barter.

1. Summer

These days, each a world
unto itself, are like the Amish
farms we drove by, the light clear,
the corners straight.

They were haying, the mowers
pulled by great, docile horses
followed by boys, their straw hats
bobbing as they bent to gather
the grass.

In the basket maker's house,
a girl, solemn as a statue,
stared at my loose hair.
Her doll had no face.
No graven images, you explained.

We drove all day, then ate
a pie baked by Ida Yoder
who added the egg whites last
which formed a crust which was savory
on our tongues.

2. Autumn

Tourists clog the roads, gawking,
snapping pictures that make the boys
in a hay loft glower, sullen
as any children anywhere. Sweet

sorghum molasses is the main
attraction. A bay mare
goes round and round grinding
stalks. Turned to pasture
would such a horse know any other path?

3. Winter

Jacob loves animals—fainting
goats, rat terriers and pigeons, prize
pigeons he'd be glad to show us.
The impressario claps his hands
and Birmingham rollers burst from the coop,
soar above the barn, then stall
and tumble toward the ground as though
suddenly, they had forgotten how to fly.

But no, it's a joke, and Jacob
and his grandsons and you and I
cannot stop laughing at acrobatic birds
and fainting goats in this peaceable
kingdom two days after Old Christmas.

4. Spring

The farm yards are empty.
No baskets today.
No peanut brittle.
Only Eli Gingrich offers
on a narrow sign KUVAS.

The roads are rutted
remnants of winter that rattle
our teeth though we make a game
from childhood humming
wild vibratos. I know

you are thinking of yesterday, our words
bubbling like the tar on summer streets.
Nothing is resolved. We abandon
language for the consolation
of light on slanted roofs.

Then, on the road to Summertown
the solid sound of hammers
and hand saw leads us to a barn raising.
A dozen or more men ride the beams—
sailors in the rigging of a ship
sailing an extravagant sky.

WRESTLING THE BEAR

It's no metaphor. It is a 700 lb. bear named Ted
brought in to wrestle drunken college boys at Club XIII,

boys who've been drinking since five and now are full
of themselves and the glory to be had if the promoter

would just stop talking: No running at the bear, no pulling
of hair. He has no claws, but yes, he does have teeth

so watch your fingers and your winkies. The bear shambles in,
and like a guy on the late shift who has learned to live

in darkness, he squints at the opposition, eyes the flesh
of the first row. And tasty it might be—the palomino

at the next table who tosses her mane in time to the music,
the lamb's wool sweater resting her breasts on the arm of a date

whose hand slides down her back like smoke. But we've come
here to watch bear wrestling and the first contestant is short,

short work for the bear, who leans on him like a refrigerator.
The next hero, a bearded Paris, is swatted to the floor. I'm pulling

for the bear as a football player, surly as Achilles,
loosens up. This kid is big; he understands torque

and he means to have the 200 bucks as he charges, twists
and the bear picks himself up shaking a cloud of hair

into the spinning light of a mirrored globe. A few more
throws and he might get mad, might jerk the tractor chain

from the puny hand of the promoter, but he knows when
to quit, knows the crowd, and anyway, has already been paid.

Later, in the grime of the trailer, the bear curls
on himself tranquilized by nicotine and the hum of tires

on the road to Athens or Chattanooga or Sparta. The promoter
counts the take, pops a top and hopes the snow holds off.

The troops straggle back to their dorms and the sky clears
above the temple where tomorrow the priests will stir

the entrails, study the portends. At home, washing
the odor of smoke from my hair, I think about Helen

back home in Sparta, where Menelaus says all is forgiven,
how silence must have fallen on her, tooth and claw.

ABOUT THE AUTHOR

Lynne Burris Butler was born and raised in Kansas. She attended the creative writing program at the University of Arkansas and taught several years at Wichita State before assuming her present faculty position at the University of North Alabama. Her previous collections are *Dream Thief* (1993) and *Forever Is Easy* (1994). Individual poems have appeared in many journals, including *Prairie Schooner, The Southern Poetry Review, The Beloit Poetry Journal,* and *The Ark River Review.* She lives in Florence, Alabama.